HISTORY'S GREATEST WARRIORS

Knights

by Kraig Helstrom

BELLWETHER MEDIA • MINNEAPOLIS, MN

Are you ready to take it to the extreme?
Torque books thrust you into the action-packed world
of sports, vehicles, mystery, and adventure. These books
may include dirt, smoke, fire, and dangerous stunts.
Warning: read at your own risk.

Library of Congress Cataloging-in-Publication Data

Helstrom, Kraig.
 Knights / by Kraig Helstrom.
    p. cm. -- (Torque : history's greatest warriors)
 Includes bibliographical references and index.
 Summary: "Engaging images accompany information about knights. The combination of high-interest
subject matter and light text is intended for students in grades 3 through 7"--Provided by publisher.
 ISBN 978-1-60014-629-9 (hardcover : alk. paper)
 1. Knights and knighthood--Juvenile literature. 2. Civilization, Medieval--Juvenile literature. I. Title.
 CR4513.H45 2012
 940.1--dc22   2011004211

Printed in the United States of America, North Mankato, MN.

080111   1187

Contents

Who Were Knights?

In **medieval** Europe, kings and **lords** fought for land and power. Knights were their **noble** warriors. They fought from horseback, commanded armies, and defended castles. They served their lords to the death.

Knight Fact

Knights often fought in single combat. This was an honorable battle between two warriors.

Knights followed a code of honor called **chivalry**. They were expected to be brave, faithful to God, and loyal to their lord. They believed in justice and fair fighting. Knights had to protect those who could not protect themselves. Some knights fought for the **Catholic Church**. They led armies during the **Crusades**.

Knight Fact

The Knights Templar was a famous brotherhood. Even the most noble knights could not join unless they proved their faith and loyalty.

Knight
Training

Boys usually became knights through **birthright**. Most were the sons of nobles. Common warriors could earn the title of knight if they proved their bravery in battle.

A boy began to train for knighthood around age 6. He first became a **page**. He learned how to ride a horse and use weapons. A knight began to teach him about chivalry.

knight

squire

page

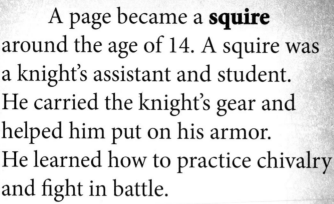

A page became a **squire** around the age of 14. A squire was a knight's assistant and student. He carried the knight's gear and helped him put on his armor. He learned how to practice chivalry and fight in battle.

Squires were usually ready to become knights around age 20. A squire was **knighted** at a big ceremony. The squire **fasted** and prayed before he was knighted. A large celebration often followed the ceremony.

Knight Fact

A squire officially became a knight after two actions. A lord had to tap him on the shoulders with a sword. Then the lord had to call him "Sir Knight."

11

Jousting: Training for Battle

Knights had to keep their fighting skills sharp. Jousting tournaments prepared them for combat.

Charge!

Two knights on horseback charged each other with wooden lances.

Winning

The winner advanced in the tournament. The loser gave his horse and armor to the winner.

Money and Prizes

A knight made money by selling his prizes back to the loser.

Scoring

A knight earned points by
striking his opponent or
knocking him off the horse.

Knight Weapons and Gear

lance

Greatswords weighed up to 10 pounds
(4.5 kilograms). Only the strongest
knights could swing them.

Knights often fought from horseback. They needed strong warhorses to ride into battle. Knights trained their warhorses to stay calm on the battlefield. Some knights covered their horses in armor. Knights on horseback fought with lances. These long, sharp weapons were made of wood and metal.

Swords were used both on the ground and from horseback. Longswords had long, narrow blades. Broadswords were wider and heavier. Greatswords were even bigger. These giant swords could bring down horses!

mace

axe

Some knights carried axes, maces, and war hammers. Axes split through enemy armor. Maces and war hammers crushed armor and broke bones.

Knights wore armor and carried shields for protection. Early knights wore chain mail. This armor was made of many small metal rings. Later knights wore plate mail made of large metal plates. Metal helmets had **visors** to protect the face. Shields were used to block enemy attacks.

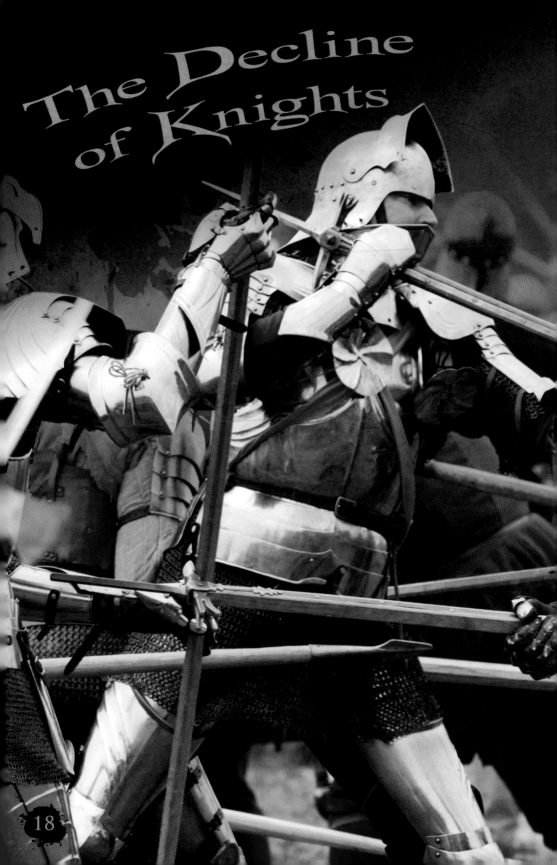

The Decline of Knights

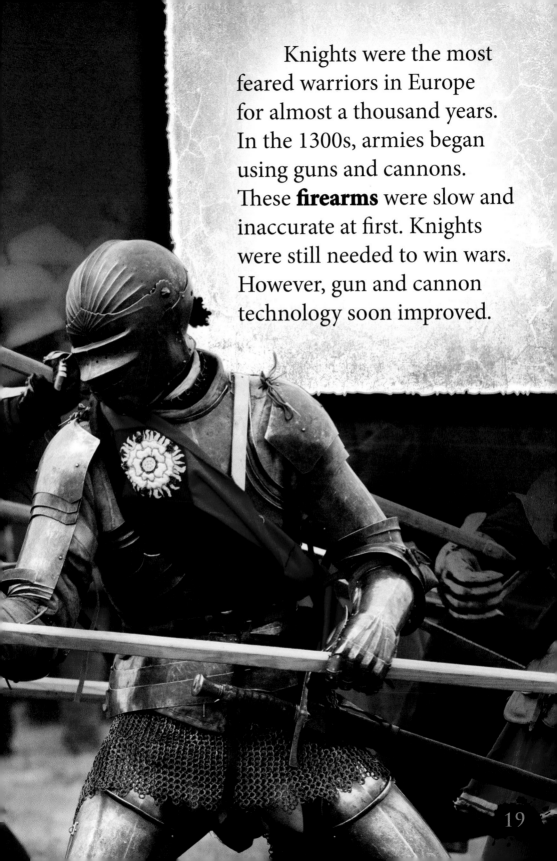

Knights were the most feared warriors in Europe for almost a thousand years. In the 1300s, armies began using guns and cannons. These **firearms** were slow and inaccurate at first. Knights were still needed to win wars. However, gun and cannon technology soon improved.

Firearms changed how battles were fought. Armies no longer relied on hand-to-hand combat. Knights could not compete with the power of these new weapons. They no longer had a place on the battlefield.

People can still be knighted today. However, the title no longer applies just to warriors. The time of armor, warhorses, and chivalry has passed. Today, those knights survive only in history and legend.

Glossary

birthright—something promised to a person because of his or her birth into a certain family or social status

Catholic Church—the world's largest group of Christians; the Catholic Church has been around for almost 2,000 years.

chivalry—a code of honor among knights; chivalry focused on bravery, loyalty, and fairness.

Crusades—military campaigns run by the leaders of the Catholic Church to win back holy lands

fasted—chose to not eat for a set amount of time

firearms—weapons that use explosions to shoot bullets or cannonballs

knighted—promoted to the rank of knight

lords—people who owned land and had high social status in medieval Europe

medieval—occurring during the Middle Ages, about 500 to 1500 CE

noble—associated with wealth, high social status, or royalty

page—the first stage of training to become a knight; pages were usually ages 6 to 13.

squire—the second stage of training for knighthood; a squire served as a knight's assistant from ages 14 to 20.

visors—moveable parts on helmets that protected the faces of knights

To Learn More

AT THE LIBRARY

Becker, Ann. *Knights and Castles*. Vero Beach, Fla.: Rourke Pub., 2010.

Dixon, Philip. *Knights & Castles*. New York, N.Y.: Simon & Schuster Books for Young Readers, 2007.

Doeden, Matt. *Weapons of the Middle Ages*. Mankato, Minn.: Capstone Press, 2009.

ON THE WEB

Learning more about knights is as easy as 1, 2, 3.

1. Go to www.factsurfer.com.

2. Enter "knights" into the search box.

3. Click the "Surf" button and you will see a list of related Web sites.

With factsurfer.com, finding more information is just a click away.

Index

The images in this book are reproduced through the courtesy of: Sibrikov Valery, front cover, p. 4; Abramova Kseniya, p. 6; Kurt Tutschek, p. 8; North Wind Picture Archives/Alamy, p. 9; World History Archive/Alamy, pp. 10-11; Stephan Goerlich/Photolibrary, pp. 12-13; Robert H. Creigh, p. 14; Nikita Rogul, p. 16 (mace); Sergii Figurnyi, p. 16 (axe); FXQuadro, p. 17; Tim Gainey, Alamy, pp. 18-19; Alex Valent, pp. 20-21.